For Jo and Tony:

**Lily**

With much love, Sue
August 12 2007

Lily knows some words that I don't know. And I don't expect you to know them either!

## About Susan Gregory

In her literary career to date, Susan has progressed from short stories written for young people and for broadcasting, through literary appreciation of Jane Austen to risqué comic verse.

She is a graduate of Oxford University and spent many years as a teacher of English.

# Lily

The memoirs in doggerel
of a late middle-aged,
somewhat overweight,
arty nymphette.

by Susan Gregory

Illustrations by Beatrice Baumgartner-Cohen

First published in 2007

Copyright © Susan Gregory 2007

ISBN 978-1-842-89010-3

All rights reserved. No part of this publication may be
reproduced or transmitted in any form or by any means,
electronic or mechanical, including photocopy, recording
or any information storage and retrieval system, without
permission in writing from the author.

Typesetting, book and cover design
by John Adler Associates, Bristol, UK.

Printed in Great Britain by Biddles Ltd, King's Lynn

Published by Pomegranate Books
3 Brynland Avenue, Bristol BS7 9DR
www.pomegranatebooks.co.uk

## Acknowledgements

I should like to say a special thank you to John Adler, whose creative suggestions and unbounded good humour have made bringing these verses to fruition a joy. Also to Beatrice Baumgartner-Cohen, whose infinite patience, seeking after perfection and visual comic sense have been an inspiration.

## List of Contents

| | |
|---|---|
| I Met a Monk | 10 |
| About Lily | 15 |
| I'm a Devil-May-Care Dilettante | 19 |
| The Crook | 22 |
| I Thought I Saw | 25 |
| The Sermon on a G-String | 26 |
| Lily Puts the Bonbons Into Her Mots | 28 |
| Lily's Manifesto | 31 |
| Paradise Mislaid | 33 |
| Drinking Song | 36 |
| Pleasure Modified | 39 |
| How Lily Flogged the Rude News of Gent (and Fakes) | 42 |
| I've Been To a Marvellous Séance | 45 |
| The Ballad of the Midriffly Challenged | 48 |
| Lily Celebrates Her Female Friends | 51 |
| Parodies Lost | 53 |
| Lily's Advice – Do Not Go Gentle Into That Face Lift | 54 |
| Lily Remembers Her Nubile Self | 56 |
| Lily Tries To Be Good | 59 |
| Lily Hits a Low Spot | 63 |
| Femina: Quis? | 65 |
| A Global Maid | 69 |
| On Comparing One's Rivals To Oneself | 71 |

| | |
|---|---|
| Lily Sings the Blues | 73 |
| Lily Stipulates Her Terms | 76 |
| Lily Contemplates the One Who'll Get Away | 79 |
| Lily's Requirements | 80 |
| The Ballad of the Jaded Courtesan | 81 |
| Shopping Song | 83 |
| Lily's Favourites | 84 |
| High Glee | 88 |
| When You are Near | 89 |
| Oh, I Can't Get You Out of My Mi-ind! | 90 |
| Lilymix | 91 |
| The Aphrodisiac Squid | 95 |
| There's Girl in the Old Life Yet | 96 |
| Lily Encounters a Few Set Backs | 97 |
| Lily the Cynic – 1 | 98 |
| Lily the Cynic – 2 | 98 |
| Upon the Tiny Lavatory | 98 |
| Lily Goes Soft-Core (and Waxes Domestic) | 98 |
| Lily – a Tribute | 99 |
| The Last Word – Ode to a Tea Cup | 100 |

To Bill and Gabbi

This manuscript was inexplicably discovered in the library of a Cistercian monastery, catalogued under 'virgin'. The only clue to its provenance is a poetic fragment found in a discarded toilet bag that once belonged to the author.

> I met a monk the other night.
> I think he was Cistercian.
> He ended up in intensive care
> Because of his exertion.

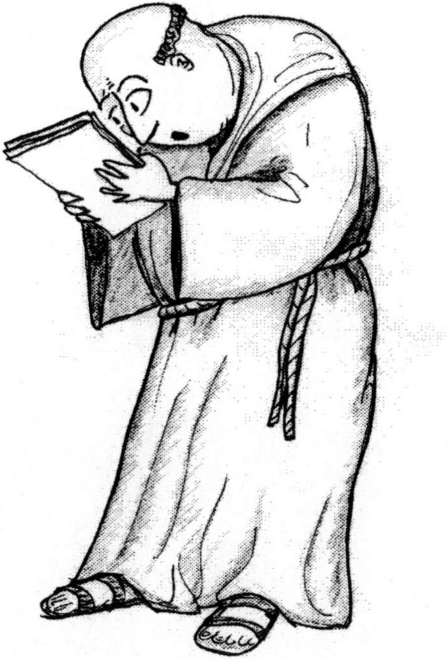

'Who is Lily? What is she?
   That all our swains adore her.....'

## About Lily

Not a lot is known about Lily. A woman of unusual taste, voracious appetite and little discretion, she once wrote:

> My poems are my legacy.
> They say it all.
> In the manner of graffiti
> On a lavatory wall.

At the age of eleven she wrote a poem, 'Second Hand Lil'. This gives an indication of her humble origins that belie her subsequent penchant for the arts, extreme sartorial elegance and men of means and endowment:

> It's second hand Lil you got here.
> These are me step-mam's shoes, me brother's socks.
> Me shirt's a second. I ain't no fashion box.
> Can't be bothered. Ain't interested in clothes,
> Shopping, money, banks....
> Got these trousers when we went to France for ten francs.
> That's me, see? Always get stuff cheap.
> Reduced everything, only sturdy, so they'll keep.
> I'll probably wear something of me dad's tomorrer.

Why waste time buying stuff when you can borrer?
But at least the ideas in me head's me own.
*I* picked 'em.
I'm no brainwashed kid. No fashion victim.

Precocious at school, Lil's passion was for poetry...
and men, in reverse order of priority. She learnt many
poems by heart, so absorbing such influences as the
heightened spirituality of John Milton, the studied
silliness of Lewis Carroll, the swashbuckling poesie
of Robert Browning, the tripping lyricism of Lord
Tennyson, the suave versification of Noel Coward and
the Celtic hyperbole of Dylan Thomas. The influence of
these men you will readily spot in this collection.

Susan Gregory

# The Lily Poems

## I'm a Devil-May-Care Dilettante

I'm a devil-may-care dilettante.
I read dirty books in the bath.
I've always been bad in a pantie
And always been good for a laugh.

I'm a devil-may-care dilettante.
I trust in my cleavage, and hope.
I live off cheap gin and Chianti
And never say boo to a grope.

I've auditioned to be a bacchante.
They think I'm as gifted as hell!
My delicto is sheer in flagrante.
(My fan dance is quite good as well.)

I've designed a new range for the bedroom
That includes importing a horse.
And I wax a *trifle* indignant
When they say that my *linen* is coarse.

My career is as varied as fore-play.
I've seen off a good many wives!
I've straddled my surfboard in Tor Bay
And brandished my brush in St Ives.

I boatht of my marthmallow fingerth.
My lithp is a put-on to teathe.
If a boy-friend thuggeth cunnilinguth
I unfailingly murmur, 'Yeth pleathe!'

I dine on deluxe cannelloni
And breakfast on beef Stroganoff.
I'm a sucker for waiters called Tony.
Can't wait till their trousers come off!

I take lashings of cream in my coffee
And dollops of whisky in milk.
My knickers are flavoured with toffee.
(Well, they'd hardly be made of pure silk.)

I've hired a régime for my body.
My instructor's no her, but a him!
If it's preluded by a hot toddy
I like to make out in the gym.

Docs look grave and say I'm a sinner
But I know, if it's left up to me,
Though I'll certainly never get thinner,
I'll live to a hundred and three!

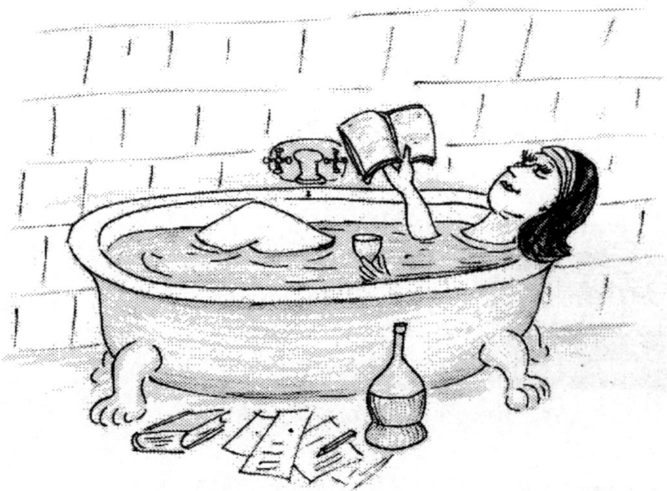

## The Crook

I come from poor and humble stock.
    I made a sudden sally.
At sweet sixteen I stopped the clock
    And escaped from our alley.

I never had a proper ma
    For childbirth proved her limit.
She said her daughter should go far
    If she had half her spirit.

By twenty I'd escaped my dad,
    A drain on my resources.
He'd always been a gambling lad
    (And mainly on the horses).

By twenty two I'd escaped town
    And found a country dwelling,
And still I kept my age right down,
    So radiant and sweet-smelling.

At last I found a farmer bold,
    And near as rich as Croesus,
Who granted me a cap of gold
    To practise safe coitus.

He would not be my husband, though,
    Which did not much surprise me,
For men may come and men may go
    And some may tantalize me.

I chatted to the village dames
    And found them most enlightening.
It seemed they shared my inner aims
    Which I found rather frightening.

For there's one Lil to strut her stuff
    And that is quite sufficient.
One femme fatale is quite enough
    If she's to be efficient.

With many a ploy I tempt my men.
    I think, to outdo father.
He'd quite a harem, way back when,
    Which, I'm sure, fuelled my ardour.

I murmur under moon and stars
    And dole out my caresses.
I take phone numbers in their cars
    And add to my addresses.

I slip, I slide, I glide, I glance
    Through all my boyfriends' coffers.
I do not leave my life to chance
    But to the highest offers.

Some men prove friend; some men prove foe,
    And some run hell for leather,
For men may come and men may go
    But I go on for ever.

### I Thought I Saw

I thought I saw a genius
   Who wrote upon a slate.
I looked again and found he was
   A rampant reprobate.
'At length I realise,' I said,
   'The bitterness of fate.'

'I want to know a laureate
   To whom I could be tethered,
To help my rhymes develop chimes
   And use the rhythm method.
He'd have to love my art because
   I'm really rather weathered.'

'My wish has been, since seventeen,
   To join the literati,
Yet every invite I have seen's
   Not for that kind of party!
Oh, why these men since, way back when,
   I've liked my fellas arty?'

## The Sermon on a G-String

Blessèd are the sloshed-on-spirits!
For thou canst carry away their menfolk on the prongs of their fish forks.

Blessèd are they that moan!
For men knoweth not if they are faking ye orgasm.

Blessèd are the bleak!
For it is easy to cheer up their loved ones with a well placed cherry.

Blessèd are they that do hunger and thirst having overdone the Atkins!
For it is easy to appear thinner than they do
By adopting a cunning disguise as an anal thermometer.

Blessèd are they with the surname Percival!
For to marry a Percival would make a nice day out
For the Woman-called-White.

Blessèd are the pure in heart!
For thou canst crucify them over a cup of cocoa.

Blessèd are the tea-makers!
Ever tried telling them their husbands are screwing
the kettle?

Blessèd are they who are prosecuted for fornicating
with toads.
For I might have a croak at it myself!

Blessèd are the reviled and those who suffer calumny,
For, lo, they are imaginative in their vengeance.
Yea, verily, I enjoy seeing manure heaped on their
detractors' drive ways
And gnomes in g-strings growing out of it in a state of
high excitement!

## Lily Puts the Bonbons into Her Mots

I was Goody Two Shoes once.
But they pinched.

If there's a glint in your eye, you don't need a diamond.

There is no such thing as going too far.
(Provided you have a first-class return ticket, of course.)

I appeal to a man's better nature.
But I always take my frock off first.

I can do anything a man can do.
But I always do it in my negligée, and sitting down.

When charming woman stoops to folly…
Applaud her initiative.

When charming woman satisfies her man completely…
Hand her an Oscar.

Today I ordered a four-wheel drive.
Well, someone has to pick up the profiteroles…

Today I waxed my bikini line.
I should have waxed indignant!

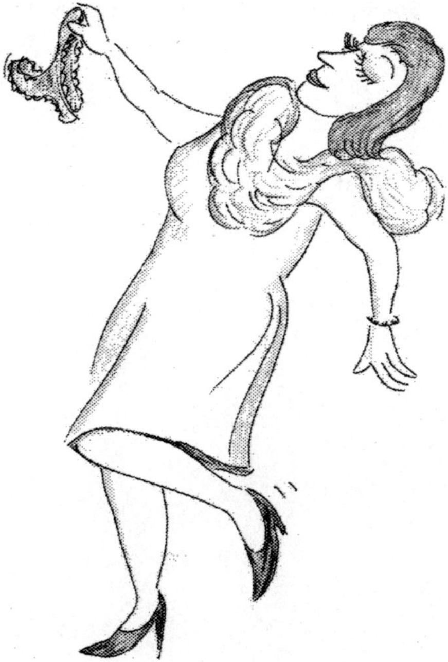

'And I can still get into my wedding dress' –
'So, where's progress?'

I'd rather fandango my way through life waving my knickers than plod through it dangling my socks!

Appear on the 'Richard and Judy Show'? I haven't the inhibitions!

Reveal my true identity? I have the cat to consider!

## Lily's Manifesto

I'm just a young and benevolent witch,
Already not steady! A terminal tease.
I've lost count of the fellows I intend to ditch
As I chassé and shimmy in my chemise.

*Refrain*

When I've got them in a lather,
Shrieking "Surely we must have her",
People tut that I've brought them to their knees.
But I am quite delightful
While they're really awfully frightful
So I'll do as I RU-DDY WELL PLEASE!

I'm just a cantankerous, rancorous maid
Born to rumble and humble the sex.
Though I like to make out that I'm really quite staid
As I launch on my mission to vex!

*Refrain*

When I've got them in a tizzy
'Cos I tell them I am busy
Gallants shriek that I am awfully unfair

But by acting kinda bashful
I find I earn a stashful
And confirm my reputation to be rare.

So they plead it as a factor
That I'm vagina intacta
And the man who tries to take me will be cursed.
Yet men think I am fantastic
'Cos my hymen's so elastic
As all embrace the celebration to be first!

## Paradise Mislaid

I come from the Garden of Eden
Without the least shadow of doubt.
I re-incarnated in Sweden
Via Paris. (I left London out.)

I hadn't much time for young Adam
And a diet of apples was tame.
He'd never have made me his Madam
And off-loaded too much of his blame.

His loving was frightfully callow
And I couldn't make fig-leaf bras stick.
His cerebral dabblings were shallow
And his apple soufflé made me sick.

He wasn't inventive with shovels
So his delving soon gave me the pip,
So I used my deep throat to blow bubbles,
Dived in there, and gave him the slip.

I think that he had a weak bladder
And his muscle tone wasn't the best.
So I took to caressing an adder
And tore up my fig leaf-of-a vest.

We set up home in a myrtle.
The view from the penthouse was great.
But I spied a *delectable* turtle
And quickly abandoned my mate!

Our off-spring were really quite other.
One called Babel. The other one Bane.
But I wasn't cut out for a mother
So I went on the apples again!

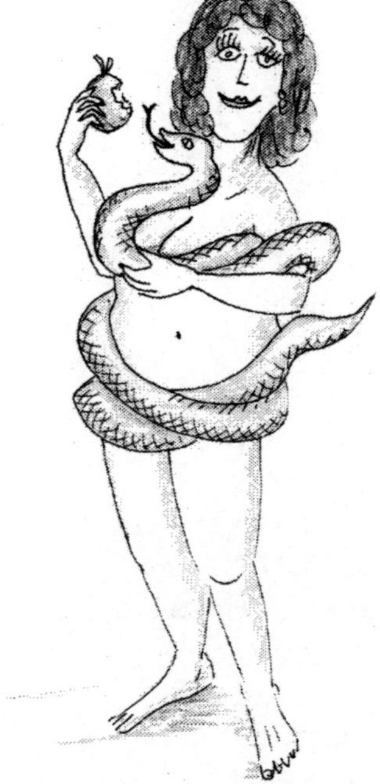

## Drinking Song

I am ogling works by Giotto
While becoming rather blotto
And am pondering who could be
A better effing muse than me!
What a face for Leonardo!
Mona Lisa with bravado.
What a subject for Da Vinci
Or a ballet by Stravinsky.
I could be the inspiration
For an Emin installation.
Or indeed a likely lass-oh
For a sculpture by Picasso.
I could not be any coarser
Than the Wife of Bath of Chaucer
And should like to make a play
For William Makepeace Thackeray!
For discerning Mr Proust
I'd provide the word most juste.
I'd be one fat masterpiece
For a collage of Matisse.
I'd bedazzle Beerbohm Tree
By my sparky repartee.

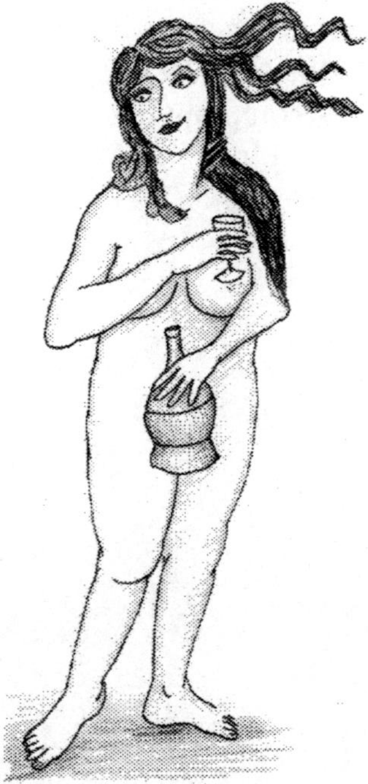

I would make a charming fresco
Or a drama by Ionesco
And a sunflower and a half
For the brush of Vince Van Gogh.
I would make a stunning nude,
Not just brains but attitude.
I would make a stirring Venus
For *any* struggling arty genius!

## Pleasure Modified

I dreamed I walked in ancient Rome
With Ovid, 'neath a moon
Of candied lemon to his home
And entered his saloon.

And there he fixed a gin and it
And wrapped me in his arms
And slid his hands around a bit.
(A toga has its charms!)

He told me tales of ravished nymphs
Who'd turned themselves to wood
And now stand petrified on plinths
To serve the common good.

The God Zeus one day turned to swan,
Took Leda in the buff,
But when she laid an egg anon
She said she'd had enough!

The story seemed to fire the bard
And I was flattered much
When he did kiss me rather hard
And called me 'chick' and such.

My instinct told me to beware
Of possible abuse.
He swore that *I* was Leda fair
And boasted he was Zeus!

With every thrust my wonder swelled
For he was such a boff
But I felt bleak when I beheld
His condom had come off!

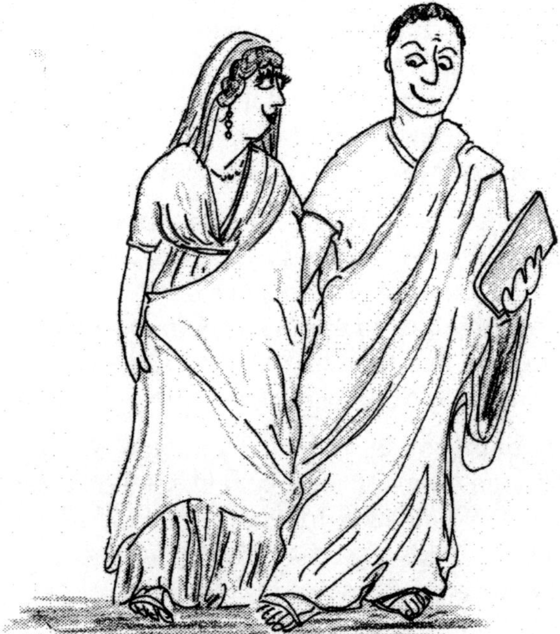

## How Lily Flogged the Rude News of Gent (and Fakes)

I sprang for the bed-post, and 'Bollocks!' quoth he!
'Let's gallop! You gallop! We'll gallop all three!'
'Take heed!' quoth a dame, as the duvet he threw
Away from her body (and revealed her in blue.)
Behind them, I shivered, not clad in too much,
(And revealing my shame, and my buttocks, and such.)

Not a word had he uttered – he's that kind of cad –
When upstairs in the darkness, (and not very clad,)
He'd silently led me, an innocent still,
Against my best judgement (if not quite my will.)
Not a clue had he dropped, not a syllable said
That the wife of the day would be sharing the bed!

I knew from my friends that he'd had quite a few.
But all thought him divorced, and in need of a new
And a nubile young lady, to whom he could hitch
All his fame and his fortune. He's frightfully rich!
And rather a catch. There we all did agree
That he warrants a snatch. He's our local MP!

Not a word to each other, his wifie and I
Berated the bastard, and wished to know why

With a couple of stunners he'd lief hit the hay,
When he'd only got married the previous day!
And we both made a pledge that, from June to September,
We'd lief disembowel our dishonourable member!

At our words, up leaped of a sudden that son
Of a bitch, and vacated the room at a run,
But we shared a resolve to harrow the hick
And united in order to track down the prick!
We sleuthed and we stalked like police on the beat,
And brained him, and fastened him in the en suite.

We shuddered at how he'd have seized with éclat
The options inherent in maisons à trois,
And blanched at the thought of escaping a spank
And the horrible, horrible heave of his flank,
And plotted to add accusations of rape
To the news that alone would leave Britain agape.

Then we laughed and we sang and we clappèd our hands
At the narrow escape from Fleur's marital bands,
And I thought how the Minister's loss was my gain
As I tossed past her tonsils his finest champagne.
Then I cast loose my tresses. She cast loose the gay
And the sweet little bows of her blue negligée.

Then, pleading exhaustion, she sank to a snooze.
(I think she had thrown back a tad too much booze.)
So I rifled her drawers, and then clad her in red
As I sat with her head 'twixt my knees on the bed,
And I tenderly grumbled how he'd been too much,
As we murmured and slumbered and solaced and… such.

### I've Been to a Marvellous Séance

I've been to a marvellous séance
And met some delectable shades.
The Medium said
That I'm brilliant in bed
And suggested they issue me grades.
We table-tapped until midnight
And tarot packed until four
And they kindly predicted when sozzled on gin
That, given my gifts, I'll be living in sin
On the Ile St-Louis with a rather large Finn.
Oh, I couldn't have enjoyed it more!

I've been to a marvellous séance.
We kept our identities mum.
I was wearing a mask
And a *rather* tight basque.
They all said they were glad I had come.
Conversation turned to the corset
And one of them proved quite a bore
For he ogled my cleavage till blue in the face
And asked why my breasts were all smothered in lace
And tried to unhook me, and swallowed his brace.
Oh, I couldn't have enjoyed it more!

I've been to a marvellous séance.
The ectoplasm was brill.
It soon took the shape
Of a rather gross ape
Which made me feel terribly ill.
We started to talk about artists
And I was quite shocked to the core
When it moved from discussion of Vince Van Gogh's ear
To go on to suggest that they tattoo my rear
With a fan by Cézanne and a doubtful Vermeer.
Oh, I couldn't have enjoyed it more!

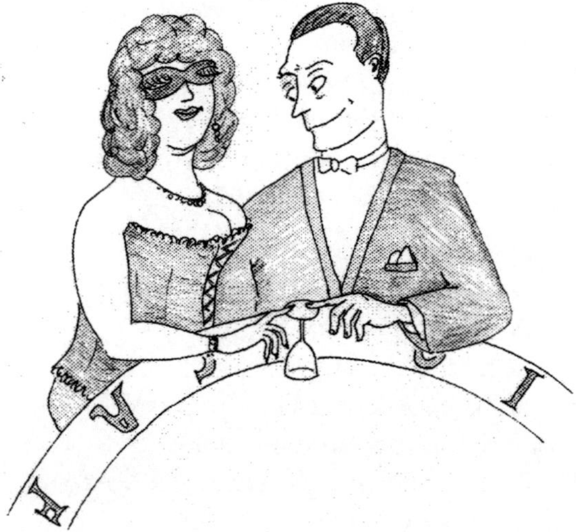

## The Ballad of the Midriffly Challenged

The bathroom scales reproach me as I strip.
I seem to have less eye and much more hip.
As I snigger at the mirror on the wall,
My lids reveal I have no eyes at all!
I ponder how on earth I can still see!
And shudder at the hipp-oh that is me.
This femme fatale's more fat-ale than she's gay.
I think I won't eat jellied eels today.

I contemplate some rhubarb and a fig.
The one's a purge; the other makes me jig!
But if I jigged from here to Timbuktu,
There'd still be more of me and less of you.
Oh, wherefore choose a lover like a rake!
A fatter one'd least give me a break!
I contemplate cream doughnuts and a coke.
For liposuction I would go for broke!

I wonder if to read would do the trick?
Divert the mind and prove that I'm not thick?
I haven't read a bloody thing at all
Of Plato, Rousseau, Kant or Juvenal.
To read of Bacchus' doings might be fun…

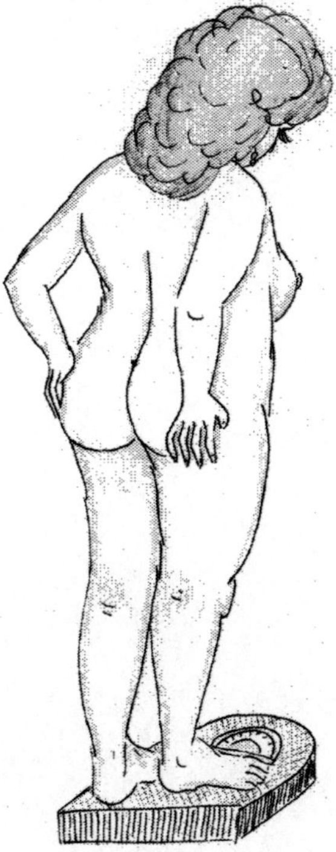

But nymphettes! Weren't they thin? And could they run!
The Classics make my varnished toe nails curl.
You could put *my* girdle three times round the world!

## Lily Celebrates Her Female Friends

In life's injurious daily round
Of 'sod its' and small damns
Where petty set-backs can confound
The least deserving lambs,
Will not a magazine improve –
'Hello' or 'Heat' or 'Vogue' –
The sorrowing bosom of the dove,
And save her from the rogue
And wretched angst that can waylay
The purest, sweetest gals?
Nay! Mags lack power to make them gay
Compared with female pals.

With female pals the cocktail hour
In riotous pleasure glides.
Shared gins in a communal shower –
There Paradise abides!
The fragrance of essential oils,
The rosy tints and hues,
The scented steam that skyward coils
Will ease away the blues.
A massage with a squishy mitt

Relaxes all our pores
And in our shower we snugly fit
Much more than out of doors.

As periods cease and bottoms droop
And seasons onward roll,
Our joie de vivre we can recoup
As we wax awfully droll
Beneath the shower head, with a glass
Of whisky or champagne.
Ah, as we sup and as we soap
We all grow young again.
What has a swain to offer gals
Compared with well oiled female pals?

## Parodies Lost

*E'en the first time Lily wed, God's wrath thunder'd
through the firmament...*

Of Lil's first disobedience, and the forbidden fruit –
A dish of mango laced with Chantilly creams –
Her husband's friend had found out were the root
Of Lil's first knowledge of post-nuptial dreams.
He'd seen her, night on night, become more bold
Till, rank on rank, her would-be suitors stood,
And some were very young, and some were very old,
And some were very suave, but none was very good.
As when a shooting star brightens the deepest reaches
Of darkness inchoate, such that the planets sing,
So the recent bride at soirées always features,
Causing many a swain to give our gal a ring,
Till the incensed friend found her beyond outrageous
When he saw her slip the marital noose again.
He feared that such behaviour could become contagious
And justify the ways of wives to men.
He prompted his friend to check the electric blanket,
As Lil prepared to entertain her guests in fives,
Thinking, 'Yea, such a gesture, all men will thank it
And justify the ways of men to wives!'

Lily's Advice -
## Do Not Go Gentle Into That Face Lift

Do not go gentle into that face lift.
See rather what night creams and unguents do
And seal with Botox what has come adrift.

Listen to the dames who have emerged quite miffed
Because they've not survived the knife brand new.
Do not go gentle into that face lift.

Wise dames, whose subtle perfumes you have sniffed,
Advise each other, and that includeth you,
'Do not go gentle into that face lift.'

For every improved face you'll find that two
Look as if they've been profoundly biffed.
Do not go gentle into that face lift.
Rage, rage against the lengthening of the queue.

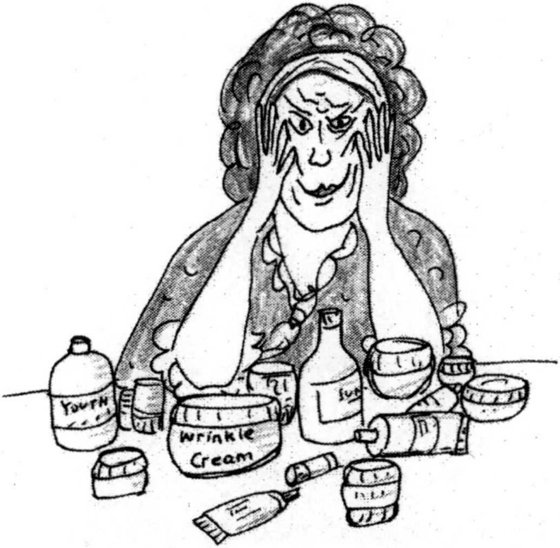
YOUTH
Wrinkle Cream

## Lily Remembers Her Nubile Self

I was not an innocenti
Tho' I was nobbut sixteen
For I knew the cognoscenti
Like to fuel a maiden's dream.

So I ordered jewels to deck me,
Lobster, furs and pink champagne,
Quite determined I would wreck my
Reputation for my gain.

For I knew the cognoscenti
Fantasize like all the rest
So I fanned their fires a plenty
To undo me while undressed!

So when lawyers praised my Latin
And took measure of my brain,
'Twixt sleek sheets of ebon satin,
I preferred it, in the main!

And when many swains had used me
And my shares began to rise,
Plastic surgery diffused my
Swelling gut and spreading thighs,

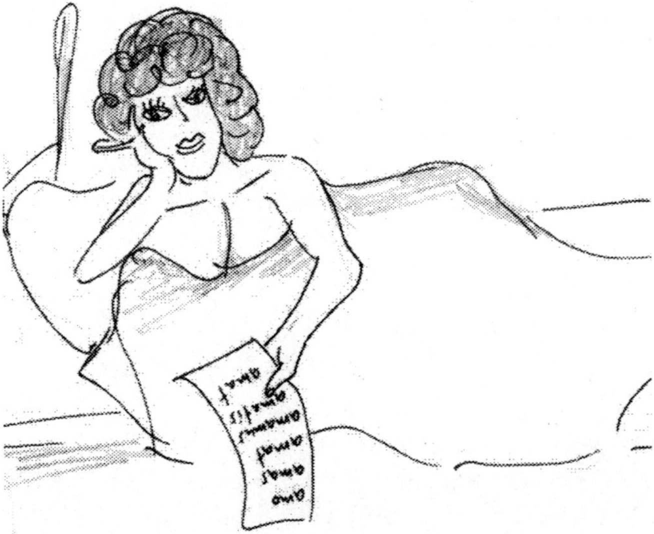
amo
amas
amat
amamus
amatis
amant

And my labia tucked and neatened,
And enhanced my stylish bum.
My imagination sweetened
At the thought of dosh to come.

And my forehead stuffed with Botox!
I considered worth the quids-
Though I suffered quite a dough-tox-
My wide-eyed stare through doctored lids!

And this brazen erstwhile maiden,
As I totted up my stash,
Knowing I was *truly* laden,
Carolled forth with flutt'ring lash:-

'I've had my bosom much inflated,
Quite prepared to wave the pain,
And my hymen reinstated,
Just to LOSE it once again!'

## Lily Tries To Be Good

My mother once told me I ought to reform,
As my habits were making her shudder,
So I took up a bed in an all female dorm
Thinking that way I couldn't be gooder.
But I'd had quite enough
When I woke in the buff
For my room mates had broken my cover.

Next I went to a milk bar in downtown LA
As I thought that the diet was wholesome.
Surely there I'd meet no-one to lead me astray
And render my prospects more dolesome?
But I spent over-long
With a gay in a thong
And a cow with a diamanté udder.

I took, with a view to acquiring more class,
An apartment in sparkling Manhattan,
But ended up sharing much more than a glass
With a very athletical Latin.
We made a great team
Upside down on a beam
At a frighteningly rhythmical judder.

I thought that some culture my prospects might mend,
As I'd suffered a surfeit of Latins,
And finally ended up in the West End
With an actor from "Timon of Athens".
But hearing his lines
Was no meeting of minds
But a prelude to something quite other.

So I found a marina quite close to St. Trope
Where the prospect was really quite sunny,
For I thought, over all, I'd be able to cope
And that hoisting a mainsail was funny.
But I went on a binge
With a tart with a fringe
And ended up arse over rudder.

I thought I might favour a man of the cloth
On account of his learned propriety,
But his sex ed. had holes, and his surplice the moth,
And he loathed my proclivities dietary.
For I'm rather extreme
With the custard and cream
And despair at an old fuddy-dudder.

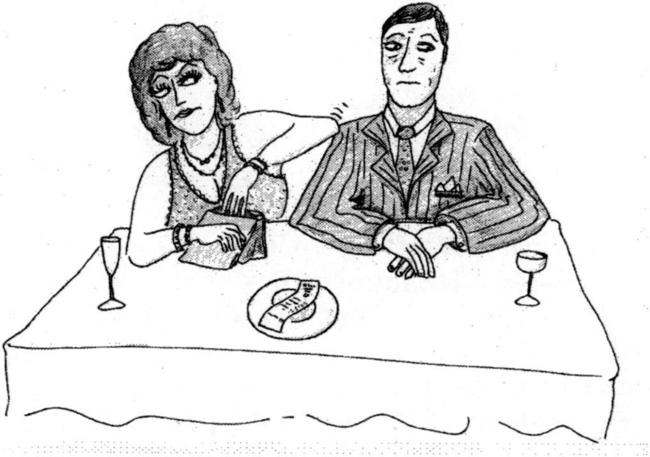

Next I looked to my assets to take some advice
From a most sympathetico banker,
Believing that bonds, shares and ISAs are nice
With the banker's rich back-up as anchor.
But there came the sad day
He insisted I pay,
That pinstriped gargoyle of a … gentleman.

I decided a course at the Sorbonne was due
And fervently studied my devoir.
I thought that prof's intellect might hold the clue,
As with Sartre and Simone de Beauvoir.
But we took to the floor at the Palais de Dance,
I did it for England,
He did it for France,
And we certainly did for my mother!

## Lily Hits a Low Spot

I'm currently low on libido.
The man of my dreams don't exist.
He's got to have brains to have credo
*And* make me explode when I'm kissed.

I dated one sold on go-getting.
A rapier wit he had not!
I was not very keen on the petting
But hot on my verbal garrotte!

Next, a predictable weirdo,
Addicted to fags and to cheese.
There wasn't much brrrrng to his brio
And his reefers inclined me to wheeze.

There was one addicted to grouting.
You'd never believe what a farce!
He never had time for an outing
And he almost sealed up my ... chimney.

Most men's intellects are quite numbing.
You'd think they'd been born in a truss.
I don't like to know what is coming!
With most it is so-o obvious!

I'm currently dating a plumpy
Who's almost surrounded by flab.
Though it isn't too bad rumpy pumpy,
Where's the cerebral grasp to his grab?

### Femina: Quis?

Thou who screwest with thy driver
Picture hooks upon my walls
Dost thou wonder what this diva
Meanest by her frequent calls?

'Come and fix my central heating.
Are you free to cut my lawn?'
Do you wonder at our meeting
Quite so oft? Yea, doth it dawn

On your tender understanding
That there's more than meets the eye
To encounters on the landing,
To my rue to say good bye?

Dearly do I love thy screwing!
I would hook thee if I could.
There is meaning in my rueing.
It smacks less of rue than rude!

Let us have a simple orgy
Here beneath the chandelier.
To proposition is quite dodgy…
Do I make my meaning clear?

Advances of a sexual nature
Would be reciprocated, though
I don't usually cater
For a man who does not know

His Rubens from his Tintoretto
Or his Beethoven from Brahms.
I am in an awful sweat. Oh,
Captivate me in your arms!

I would lief be *really* hammered
By a man who knows his stuff
Than have coy endearments stammered.
Let me seize my bit of rough

And ready workman-like bonanza.
My essential artisan!
A complete orgazmizanza
Celebrates the rights of man

And of woman. God defend her
From the prudes who'd do her down
And deny her right to wend her
Wayward way from town to town.

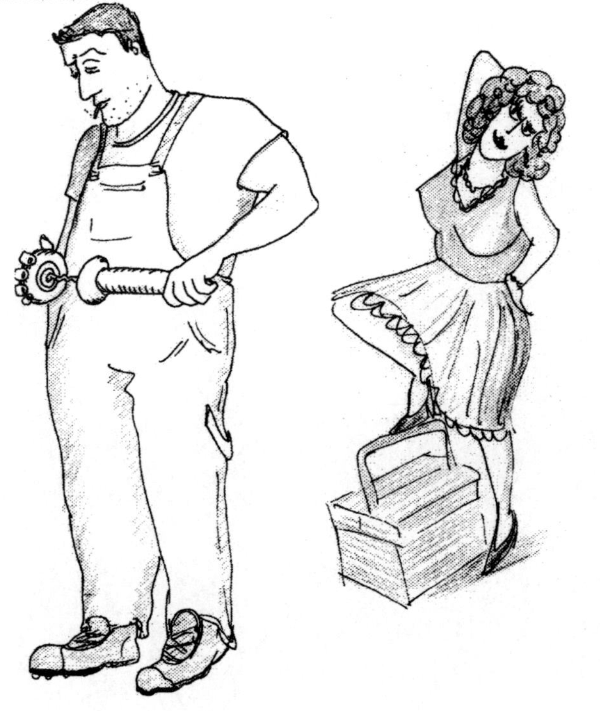

She would flee from Queen and country.
She is eager! She is game!
She would take on all and sundry.
'De rigeur' sounds awfully tame

When compared with seizing freedom
Or a workman's denims' zip!
Quis est femina? Et quis,
In wondrous coitus, DON'T LET RIP?

## A Global Maid

Oh I'm a global maid
Of the demi-monde.
Of the roué and the blade
I am awfully fond!
I'm one soignée dame,
Even when I'm tight!
And though a tad to blame
I am not contrite!
When I'm rather boozed,
I'm wholesome still, and pure,
And though a *trifle* used
I am still demure.
Husbands – I've had a few,
But transpire what may,
I'm quite an ingénue
In my global way.
I always spurn the callow.
(Worldly is more real.)
As for the straight and narrow,
It really don't appeal.

I am only using my sense
Wanting not to be a wife.
I shall plead poetic license
In the after-life.

### On Comparing One's Rivals to Oneself

Three tears for Marilyn.
Her breasts were large,
Her psyche thin.

And what of our Marlene?
Her larynx lush,
Her sheets, not clean!

How good was Mae's technique?
Her quips pure sun,
Her Latin, weak.

And then there's Miss Gabor.
Her boas, fluff,
Her eye-sight, poor.

Hélas, Brigitte Bardot!
Her pussies thrived,
Her love-life, no.

And what of Spicy Posh?
Her diet works.
Her judgement? Gosh!

Is Jordan over-rated?
Her ego's great.
Her assets, much inflated!

And what of Lily White?
Her CV's strong.
Her thighs, not light!

## Lily Sings the Blues

I'm currently infatuated
With a rather pure young man.
I'm awfully glad he was created.
I'm his biggest fan.

It is awfully chaste, my sleeping.
I bewail it day by day.
It is such a waste of weeping.
But I do it anyway.

It is such a meagre diet,
Fantasising on his rear.
My libido's running riot
But I keep a pure veneer.

He is into global warming
And as green as green could be.
Consid'ring melting poles a warning
Doesn't leave much time for me!

He is keen to tackle carbon.
I am keen to tackle him!
But the major thing he's hard on
Is globe trotting on a whim.

And I am the worst offender
When I fly to Cannes for lunch.
E'en for him I won't surrender
Travel, if push comes to crunch.

There's no pause like Harold Pinter's
In my vast itinerary.
In Prague I like to spend my winters
And my summers in Capri.

He's a government adviser
All emissions to de-tox.
I am trying to devise a
Way he'll think outside the box.

He is being my consultant
On an eco-friendly home.
I am feeling quite exultant
As I grant him right to roam!

Though his scruples undermine me –
He berates me hour by hour –
I shall make quite sure he finds me
Saving water in the shower!

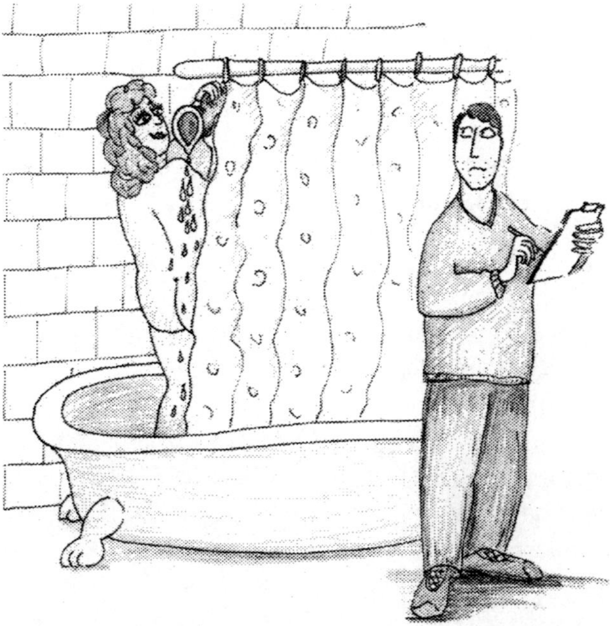

## Lily Stipulates Her Terms

When I consider
The highest bidder
For my libid-d-er

I firmly stipulate
A rich sophisticate,
No wimpy in-cho-ate.

He must be cute and droll
And rather beautiful,
Above all, DUTIFUL.

Oh, the man that I seek
May be rather antique
But as long as he has bags of BOOTY
He can dictate terms
Provided he learns
That a fella must fulfil his duty.

Oh, he may have no hair,
Or be debonair,
Or futile or balmy or fruity,
But Lily expects,
With the deepest respects,
Each fella to fulfil his duty.

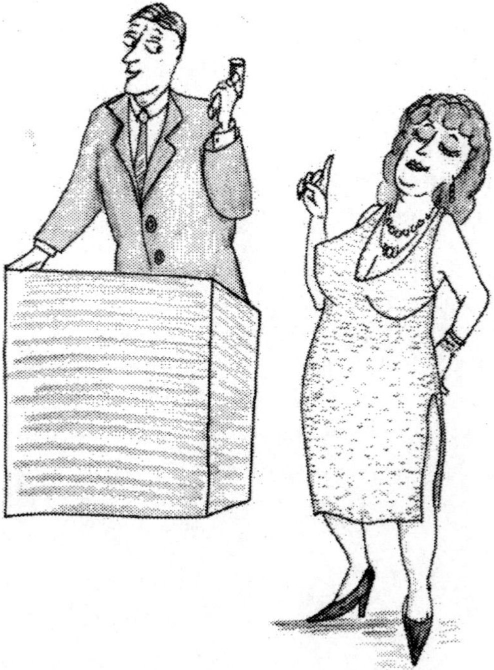

He may be-e-e
Up the creek,
Or down the pan,
Or high as the sky
On diazepam.

He may-ee incur regret
Or the National Debt,
Or tickets for two on a Jumbo Jet,

But Lily expects
With the deepest respects,
Each fella to fulfil his duty.

## Lily Contemplates the One Who'll Get Away

He is poor but he is cultured.
He can talk and he can think.
But his liver's awfully vultured
By the demon beak of drink.

Still, he is an intellectual
And I pine for brainy men,
Though he's rendered ineffectual
When he's in an opium den.

When the wreathing poppy tames him
And on spirits he is high,
How my cerebellum claims him!
How I long to stroke his thigh!

Yet I think I must eschew him
Though I hate to seem a bore
When I hanker to undo him
There's a snag I can't ignore.

Though he's one colossal looker,
Though his student stomach's flat,
He mistakes me for his hookah.
Who can hack a thing like that?

## Lily's Requirements

I do not seek renown.
I am no snob.
But when the chips are down,
I scorn the mob.

*Refrain*: Oh, I'd gladly grant a kiss
To a debonair Marquis!

My tastes are plain.
Rank is a bore.
I do not aim for gain,
Only for more!

*Refrain*: Oh, my bosom I would bare
For a rather well-heeled Herr!

I'm the simplest of girls.
No way I'm fine!
But choose to cast my pearls,
At seigneurs, not swine.

*Refrain*: Oh, I would lose my … mind
For one suitably refined!

## The Ballad of The Jaded Courtesan

Eye-lash flutterin'
Gives me tics.
Roguish smilin'
Strains the lips.
Buttock swivellin'
Makes me squirm.
Coys-'n-come-ons,
Contradictions in terms!
Bosom heavin'
Is a strain.
Breast revealin'
Taxes brain!
Gown descendin'
Makes me shiver.
Champagne toastin'
Rots the liver.
Breeches droppin'
Makes me bleak.
There's no stoppin'
For a week!
Fakin's borin',
Comin's Scotch mist.

*Try* allurin'
When you're pissed!

## Shopping Song

When I've got men on the hop
(Whip dilly-dally-oh!)
I've a tendency to shop
(Fiddle-faddle folly-oh!)
It may be a pretty frock
(Oh Marshall and Snell-gro!)
Or a fetching hunk of rock
(Oh twinkle- twankle oh!)
Or a leopard skin chaise longue
(Oh Waring and Gill-oh!)
Or a diamanté thong
(Oh Crikey! Billy-oh!)
And when I want a break
(Oh Kardomah Café oh!)
I've a tendency to cake
(No, Mr Kipling, no!)
Oh, when I'm feeling penal
(Thwack-groany oh-doh!)
My inclination's to the venal!
(Oh, Jaeger! Cartier! Oh!)

## Lily's Favourites

I like to rise at noon
When I've drunk a keg.
A little luncheon on a tray,
A little plover's egg.

Then drive out in the Rolls
And frolic in the park,
A little poodle at my heels,
All fluff, and little bark.

And sup a cup of tea
At a bijoux hostelry
And sojourn in my bower
Until the cocktail hour.

Then have a coupla gins
And a rather fruity Pimms
On some rosy balcon-ee
Where someone else will pay the fee.

Then go out upon the town
In a rather sumptuous gown,
Sporting an exotic flar
While I toy with caviar.

And calculate my gain
While I toss back the champagne
Then after Aylesbury duck
Retire and have a ….

read.

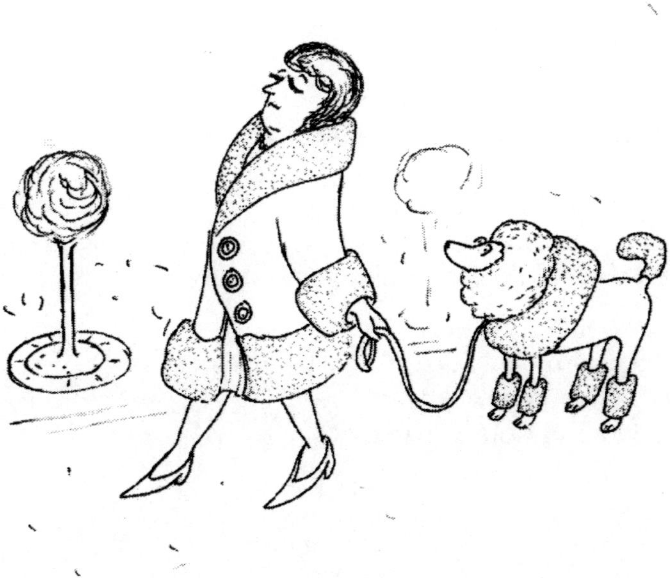

## High Glee

Come up and see my syncopation
(I can Charleston with the best,)
And jazz up my circulation
As I boogie in my vest.
We'll be very flappy,
Jitterbugging more and more,
And supremely happy, on the bathroom floor.
We will do it hourly!
Never mind if people find
That we're a bore.
We'll be very flowery, making love, not war.

I can't believe my luck!
As I play it by the book,
I feel surely fated
To be rombustiously mated!

## When You Are Near

When you are near
It's daffodil time in the Dales,
And my dream topping never fails.
The ten-sixteen goes off the rails!
When you are near.

When you are near
The planets twirl in two-four time.
I do not crave a single dime,
And something happens to my rhyme
When you are near.

When you are near
My tootsies melt like toasted cheese
And birds are flirting with the bees.
Oh, let me be your strawberry tease!
When you are near…

## Oh, I Can't Get You Out of My Mi-Ind!

Oh, I can't get you out of my mi-ind…
You are tangled in the mangle
As I execute the laundry or explore the
Butcher's slab or the grocer's groaning shelves.
I am thinking of our naked selves.
I cannot fake it. You can take it as you please
For you are the rooster's knees!
I can't rue the
Day I saw you as I hoover
And remove the fluff out of my
Navel, in the buff, before the mirror.
I'm in a dither as I slither through the railings
On a short cut to the station
And my imagination's
A fascination
When I'm running for the bus…

And oh, the careless rapture when at last we're
Snuggled in the ruggle,
Head over heels in US!

## Lilymix

There was a young person from Ealing
Who gave Lil's bottom a feeling.
She cried, "I have class
So please unhand my ass.
You are setting my cami-knicks reeling."

There was a young gallant from Leicester
Who kissed Lil as though he'd digest her
But she let it rest
'Cos she was impressed
By the panache with which he undressed her.

A dashing young sailor from Dover
Disembarked to give Lil the once over.
He thought her so nice
That he did it twice,
That importunate sailor from Dover.

A struggling young sculptor – a Chilean,
Thought Lily was one in a million.
On seeing the facts
He set about her with wax
And soon gave our dear Lil a Brazilian.

There was a young person from Wapping
Who claimed to eclipse Lily's shopping.
So her dresses she spread
In a pile on the bed
And suggested they made a dream topping.

There was an old vicar from Chester
Who frowned at Lil's habits and blessed her.
She was so shocked
That she got him defrocked,
That lucky old cleric from Chester.

An old barman from dear Lily's local
Scanned her cleavage through lenses bifocal.
He claimed that that way
He saw four breasts a day
In praise of which he was most vocal!

A charming young fellow from Tesco
Is currently painting a fresco.
He drives Lily wild
As Madonna (with child)
When she'd far rather play Manon Lescaut!

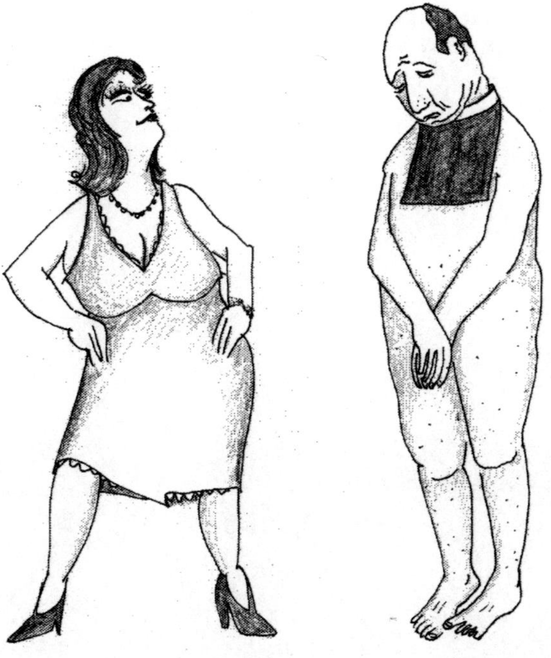

There was a young medic from Goring
Who waxed most exceeding adoring
But Lil couldn't cope
With his cold stethoscope,
A factor she found very boring.

### The Aphrodisiac Squid

When they're feeling rather rude,
Men ask me out to share their food,
But, before I clinch a venue,
I always ask what's on the menu.
If gallantry is not quite dead
I can end up demurely fed,
But if they're featuring their id
They leer at me and murmur, 'Squid.'
If *squid's* an aphrodisiac,
I want my fellas hanging slack!

## There's Girl In the Old Life Yet

Oh I should like to take to drink,
A roaring, reeling lush!
And sozzle till I thailed to fink
And end up in a bush!
Imbibing vodka until when
I fell on my behaind
But I am taking to the pen,
For I am so refained.

## Lily Encounters a Few Setbacks

A young mechanic from Woking
Is giving the Bentley a poking.
He's prepared to render my motor his best
But refuses to service *my* interest.

A handsome young farmer called Ramon
Refuses to visit my salon.
He's desperately interested in horse manure
But he's not given to lit-er-a-ture.

A striking young gardener from Dorking
Is giving the dung heap a forking,
But when I suggest that he sow a few oats
He declares that old dames offer nought to young goats.

An enchanting young fellow from Ely
Has rendered my gains touchy-feely.
Though he's given my bonds and my shares quite a lift
My *vital* statistics are left all adrift.

A randy old buffer from Reading
Looks as if for the grave he is heading
But when I suggest we give marriage a chance
He says that would rob life of all its romance.

### Lily the Cynic – 1

Though my passion's evident,
Importunate, unruly,
Immediately all passion's spent,
I am *not* yours truly!

### Lily the Cynic – 2

Although you've almost all your hair,
Although your voice is whispery,
I sometimes murmur in despair,
'I wonder what's in this for me?'

### Upon the Tiny Lavatory

Upon the tiny lavatory
The sozzled Lily lies.
("I tried to raise my dignity…
But got trapped by my thighs!")

### Lily Goes Soft-Core (and Waxes Domestic)

I'm prepared to plump up your eider.
I'd toss back your duvet with glee.
And I'd swop a whole *barrel* of cider
For a flagon of Horlicks, and thee.

## Lily – A Tribute

The world has known great women
As everyone would agree.
But none compare - she is so rare -
With risible Miss Li-lee.

The clever men at Oxford
From Nash to Oscar Wilde
Are quite prepared (when she is bared)
To grant themselves defiled!

The Eskimos in the Arctic
When they are almost froze
Are known to bring their... TEMPERATURE ... up
By rubbing Lily's nose.

Our boys, when in hot trouble,
A-fighting Blighty's wars
Exert their will (or even KILL)
For a glimpse of Lily's drawers.

Prince Charles, when with Camilla,
Exclaimed, much to her fright,
'Who is that dame who looks quite game?
Good God! It's Lily White!'

The Last Word –
**Ode to a Tea Cup**

In love I always over-stretch
Then twang to base and want to retch,
But when I court catastrophe
There's always early morning tea.

Though my behaviour grows much worse
I can't quite grasp why there's a fuss.
Whatever sweetmeats love may bring
Early morning tea's the thing.

Although I'm getting on a bit
I find love's bonfires always lit
But know that if I lose my looks,
There's always early tea, and books.

Most days I thrill, most days I pine
And fuel my grin with gin and wine
But beyond love there'll always be
That all-enduring cup of tea.

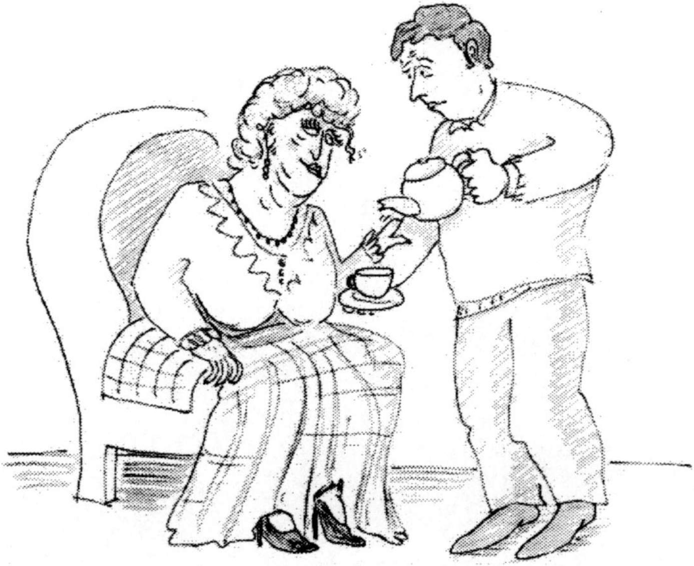